HOW TO GROW

# Potato Chips

By Alix Wood

Ruby Tuesday Books

**Published in 2024 by Ruby Tuesday Books Ltd.**



Editors: Ruth Owen & Mark J. Sachner
Design: Emma Randall & Alix Wood
Production: John Lingham

Photo credits:
Alamy: 18T (Andia); NASA: 11B; Ruby Tuesday Books: 7B, 8T, 9, 11T, 12–13, 15T, 21; Shutterstock: Cover (Pixel-Shot/Mary Valery/FotoDuets/various), 4 (AS Foodstudio/Joe Gough/Philip Kinsey/Hekla/PIXbank CZ/Gita Kulinitch Studio/Marilyn Barbone/Tiger Images), 5 (Beto Santillan), 6 (Diyana Dimitrova/Elena Zajchikova/Alexeysun), 7T (Vinokurov Alexandr), 8B, 10 (Elena Zajchikova), 14T (ESOlex/Graham Corney/Suede Chen), 15C (Nataliia Kuznetcova), 15B (Tomasz Klejdysz), 16 (Kalinin Ilya), 17 (ArieStudio), 18B (FotoDuets), 19 (Leitenberger Photography), 20 (Kenneth William Caleno/Ninell/R Villalon), 22 (Olko 1975/IZF/Berna Namoglu), 23 (golubka57/Chad Hutchinson/Gv Image-1/Sanlyn).

Library of Congress Control Number: 2023952424

Print (Hardback) ISBN 978-1-78856-353-6
Print (Paperback) ISBN 978-1-78856-354-3
ePub ISBN 978-1-78856-356-7

Published in Minneapolis, MN
Printed in the United States

**www.rubytuesdaybooks.com**

# Contents

Boil them, mash them, or bake them in their jackets. We eat potatoes in lots of ways. We can also turn them into hash browns, French fries, and crunchy

**POTATO CHIPS.**

There are around 5,000 different types of potatoes!

Potatoes grew as a wild plant in South America.

The Incas of Peru were the first people to grow them as a food **crop**.

Potatoes from Peru

The Incas even used the time it took to cook a potato as a measurement of time.

Many plants **reproduce** by growing **seeds**. Potato plants make new plants by growing **tubers** under the ground.

Rows of potato plants on a farm

The potatoes we eat are actually a potato plant's tubers. Each one can become a new plant.

Potatoes have small, lumpy parts that people call "eyes." Each eye is a **bud** that can become a new **shoot**.

## The best time to start growing potatoes is in the spring.

You can buy potatoes called "seed potatoes" from a garden center or online. Or you can use potatoes from your kitchen.

### YOU WILL NEED:

- An egg carton
- 6 egg-sized potatoes
- A large container (see page 8 for ideas)
- Potting soil
- Scissors
- A small garden trowel
- A watering can
- A bucket
- A paper bag or small cardboard box

Seed potatoes have been specially grown and cared for to make sure they grow into healthy plants.

1. Carefully examine your potatoes to see which end has the most eyes or buds.

2. Rub off any buds on the other end.

3. Put a potato in each compartment of the egg carton. The buds should be on top.

4. Place the carton in a light, cool spot, and wait for the buds to grow into shoots.

Getting potatoes to grow shoots is known as "chitting."

Your potatoes will take about four weeks to grow shoots. Then they are ready to be planted.

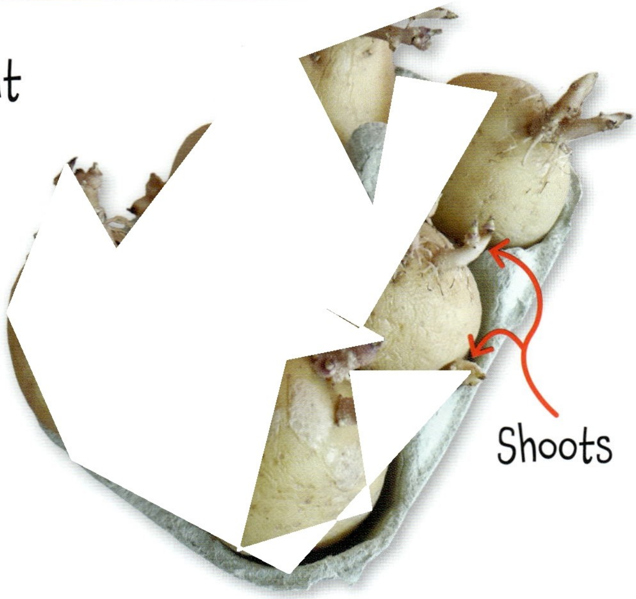


Potatoes can be grown in the ground or in a large container.

**1** Choose a container for your potato plants. You can use a big flowerpot or bucket, or a plastic storage box, as long as it's not see-through.

**2** Make sure the container you choose has drainage holes in the bottom. This allows any extra water to drain away.

If you use a plastic box or bucket, ask an adult to make holes with a drill or ice pick.

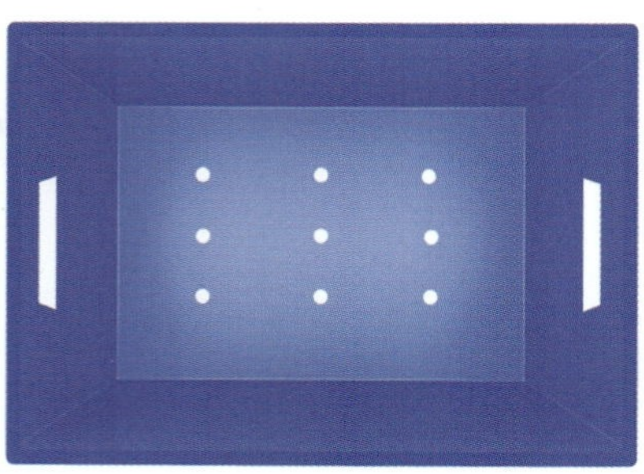

**3** Place the container outside in a sunny position.

**4** Carefully cut open the bag of potting soil. Fill your container one-quarter full of soil.

**5** Choose the two potatoes with the most shoots and place them on top of the soil. Make sure the shoots are at the top and the potatoes are at least 8 inches (20 cm) apart.

You can plant your other potatoes in different containers or give them to a friend to grow.

**6** Cover the potatoes with 2 inches (5 cm) of soil.

**7** Water the potatoes so the soil is moist when you touch it, but not soggy.

Always wash your hands with warm water and soap after working with soil.

# The Plants Start to Grow

Under the warm, damp soil, the potatoes will grow **roots** and shoots. After about three weeks, the shoots will appear above the soil.

The potato plants' leaves start to make a sugary food for energy. They do this using water, **carbon dioxide** gas from the air, and sunlight.

A potato plant's roots take in water and **nutrients** from the soil.

When leaves use sunlight to make food, the process is called photosynthesis.

## As your potato plants grow, they will need a little care.

**1** Keep checking to see if the plants need water. If the soil is dry, water the plants so the soil is moist.

**2** As your plants grow, other unwanted plants known as **weeds** may grow, too. Carefully pull out any weeds from the container.

Weeds can be tough and fast-growing. They will take water and nutrients from the potato plants.

Space shuttle

In 1995, a space shuttle blasted off with some potato plants onboard. The plants survived in space and actually grew some small potatoes!

## As the plants grow above ground, tubers start to form underground.

Under the soil, stems called stolons grow from the plant's main stems.

Some of the food made by the plant's leaves moves to the end of each stolon.

The food becomes a substance called starch.

The end of each stolon swells up with starch and becomes a tuber, or new potato.

To help your plants grow more tubers, you now add extra soil to the container. This is called hilling, or earthing up.

1. Once the leafy plant is 10 inches (25 cm) high, it is ready to be hilled.

2. Carefully add handfuls of potting soil around your plants. Bury the stems and leaves, until there are just a few leaves showing.

The buried leaves will become part of the soil.

3. Now the part of the plant's stem that has been buried will also grow stolons. Each stolon will produce a potato tuber.

4. As your plants grow, keep hilling them until the soil reaches almost to the top of your container.

Do you have a compost heap or know someone who does? You can mix some compost with the soil when hilling your plants to give them extra nutrients.

Once your potato plants are two to three months old, they will produce purple or white flowers.

As your plants grow, keep checking for signs of disease or an attack from **pests**.

Potato blight is a **fungus** that damages and kills potato plants. Cut off and throw away any leaves with signs of potato blight.

Potato blight

Click beetles are insects that lay their eggs in soil near potato plants. After about four weeks, **larvae**, known as wireworms, hatch. They tunnel into the tubers and feed on them.

1 To find out if your soil has wireworms, try this clever trick. Push a piece of raw potato onto a skewer.

2 Bury the potato in the container with the skewer sticking out of the soil.

3 Every two to three days, pull the potato trap from the soil and check for feeding wireworms.

4 Remove any wireworms you find from the container.

Put the wireworms in a place where birds will find them and get a tasty snack.

5 Look for more wireworms by digging in the soil with a garden trowel. Do this gently and carefully so you don't disturb the tubers.

# It's Harvest Time!

As your potato plants and their flowers start to die, all the plants' energy goes into the underground tubers. The tubers, or potatoes, grow bigger and bigger.

Now it is time to harvest your potatoes!

If potato tubers are left in the ground, they detach from their stolon stems.

Each tuber is now packed with starchy, energy-giving food.

A tuber can use this energy to grow new roots and shoots, and become a whole new potato plant.

**1** To harvest some potatoes, use a small garden trowel to gently remove some of the soil from the container. Put the soil into a bucket.

**2** Now comes the fun part! Using your hands, feel in the soil for potato tubers. The potatoes should be at least 1 inch (2.5 cm) across.

If they are smaller, replace the soil and leave for another week.

Some tubers, like these, may still be connected to the plant. Others may be loose in the soil.

**3** Using your hands, lift out any potatoes that are the right size. Harvest just what you want to eat and leave the rest in the soil.

Brush or wipe any soil from the potatoes. Store them in a paper bag or cardboard box in a dry, dark place.

On a potato farm, machines are used to plant and harvest thousands of potatoes.

A tractor pulls a potato-planting machine.

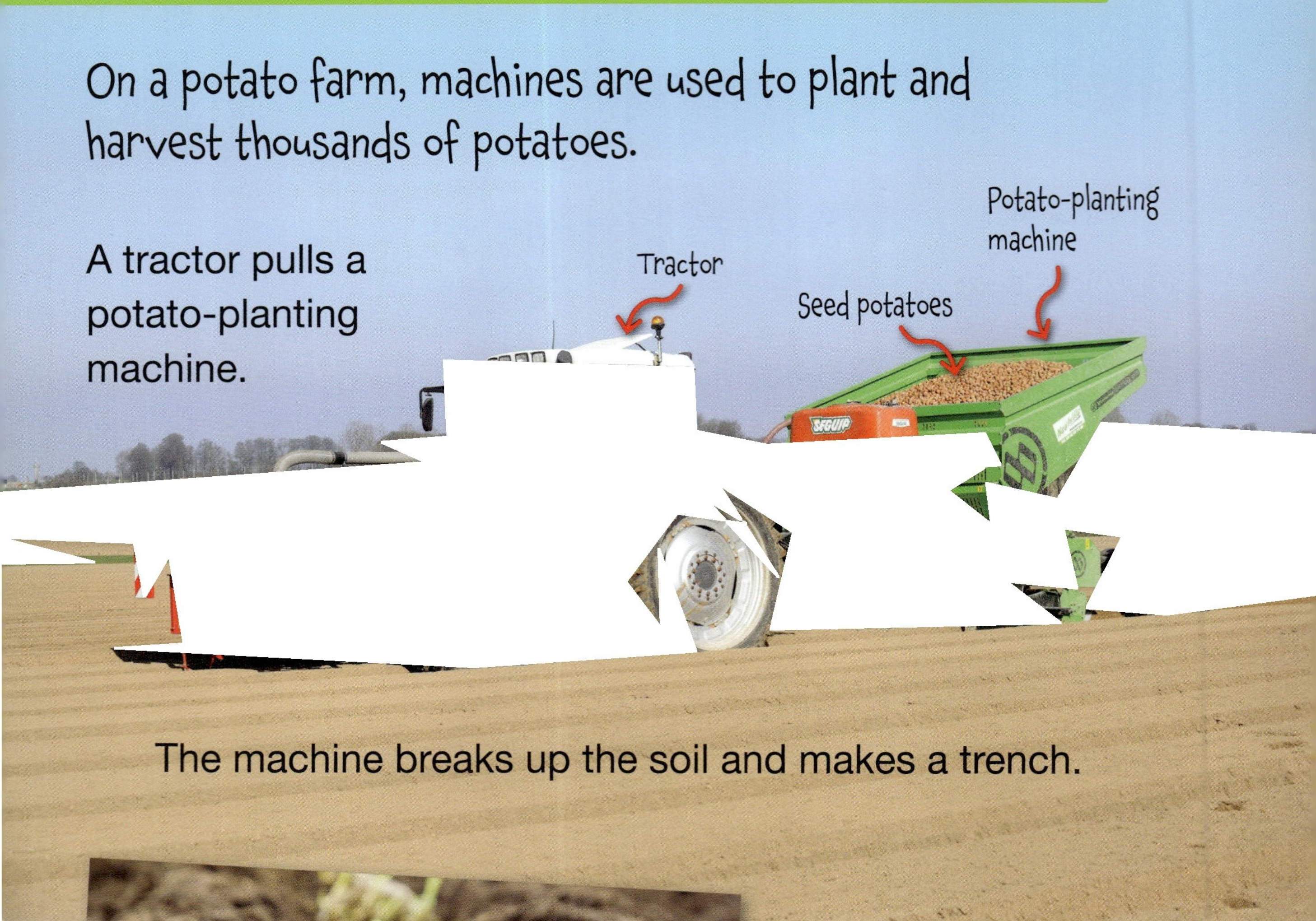


The machine breaks up the soil and makes a trench.

The machine drops seed potatoes, one by one, along the trench.

Finally, blades drag soil over the seed potatoes and fill the trench.

A potato-harvesting machine is used to harvest the crop.

The machine digs into the soil below the potatoes.

The machine lifts soil and potatoes onto a conveyor belt that has metal bars and spaces.

Any rocks and the soil fall through the spaces between the bars.

The potatoes travel along the conveyor belt and fall into a trailer.

If you enjoy a snack of potato chips, you can make this treat with your homegrown potatoes.

**BE SAFE!**

Make sure an adult helps with the cutting and is there to help you when you use the oven.

## YOU WILL NEED:

**Ingredients**
- 2 or 3 small or medium-sized potatoes
- 3 tablespoons olive oil
- Salt

**Equipment**
- A small scrubbing brush
- Paper towel
- An adult helper
- A vegetable slicer or sharp knife and cutting board
- A baking sheet
- A pastry brush
- Oven mitts
- A potholder or hot pad
- Kitchen tongs or a spatula

1. Preheat the oven to 400°F (200°C). Scrub the potatoes in warm water and pat them dry with paper towel.

2. Next, using a knife or vegetable slicer, ask your adult helper to cut the potatoes into VERY thin slices.

You can peel your potatoes or leave the skins on.

3 Brush the baking sheet with a thin layer of olive oil. Lay the potato slices on the sheet. Make sure there is space around each slice.

4 Brush a thin layer of oil onto each potato slice. Sprinkle with salt.

5 Wearing oven mitts, put the baking sheet into the oven and bake the chips for 10 minutes.

6 Carefully remove the sheet from the oven and place on a potholder or hot pad. Using tongs or a spatula, turn each chip over. Remember! They will be super hot.

7 Put the sheet back into the oven and bake the chips for another 2 to 5 minutes. Keep watch! They will cook quickly. You want them crispy, but not burned.

8 Remove the potato chips from the oven, allow to cool, and enjoy.

**bud**
A small part on a plant that grows into a new shoot, leaf, or flower.

**carbon dioxide**
A colorless gas in the air that plants use to make food.

**crop**
Plants, such as vegetables or fruit, that are grown in large numbers, often on a farm.

**fungus**
A type of living thing, such as a mushroom, toadstool, or mold.

**larvae**
The young of some insects, such as flies and beetles.

**nutrients**
Substances needed by a plant or animal to help it live and grow. For example, magnesium is a nutrient that helps potato plants grow bigger tubers.

**pest**
An insect or other animal that feeds on crops or damages them.

**reproduce**
To make more of a living thing.

**roots**
Underground parts of a plant that take in water and nutrients from the soil.

**seed**
A tiny part of a plant that contains all the material needed to grow a new plant.

**shoot**
A new part of a plant. Shoots grow from seeds and tubers.

**tuber**
An underground part of a plant that stores food for the plant. Shoots and new plants grow from tubers.

**weed**
A wild plant that is growing where it is not wanted. Weeds are tough and usually grow quickly.

## Read More

**Owen, Ruth**. *Fruits and Vegetables: How We Grow and Eat Them (Get Started With STEM)*. Minneapolis, MN: Ruby Tuesday Books (2022).

**Wood, Alix**. *How to Grow Carrot Cake*. Minneapolis, MN: Ruby Tuesday Books (2024).